To Our Grandparents, We Want to Hear Your Story

A Grandparents' Shared Memory Journal To Share Their Lives & Their Love

Jeffrey Mason

Hear Your Story Books

"Life
can only
be understood
backwards;
but it must
be lived
forwards."

– Soren Kierkegaard

This Is the Life Story of

_____

&

_____

Paste
A Photo
Here

TABLE OF CONTENTS

"Being someone's first love may be great. But to be their last is beyond perfect."

- Author Unknown

How We Became Mr. & Mrs.

The First Time We Met...

The first time we met each other was on this date...

_____

_____

This is where we were...

_____

_____

_____

This is who we were with...

_____

_____

_____

_____

_____

_____

_____

The First Time We Met...

The story of how we met is...

_____

_____

_____

_____

_____

_____

_____

_____

_____

_____

_____

Her Memories of the First Time We Met

I was this age when we first met...

_____

This is what was going on in my life during this time...

_____

_____

_____

_____

_____

_____

_____

_____

_____

_____

Her Memories of the First Time We Met

If my memory is right, this is what I was wearing...

_____

_____

_____

_____

_____

And this what I remember him wearing...

_____

_____

_____

_____

_____

_____

Her Memories of the First Time We Met

My first impressions of him were...

_____

_____

_____

_____

_____

_____

_____

_____

_____

_____

_____

_____

Her Memories of the First Time We Met

This is the first thing I remember him saying to me...

_____

_____

_____

_____

And this is what I remember us talking about...

_____

_____

_____

_____

Other details I remember about that moment include (examples to include could be a song that was playing, the weather, or who you were with)...

_____

_____

_____

_____

_____

_____

His Memories of the First Time We Met

I was this age when we first met...

_____

This is what was going on in my life during this time...

_____

_____

_____

_____

_____

_____

_____

_____

_____

_____

His Memories of the First Time We Met

If my memory is right, this is what I was wearing...

_____

_____

_____

_____

_____

And this is what I remember her wearing...

_____

_____

_____

_____

_____

His Memories of the First Time We Met

My first impressions of her were...

_____

_____

_____

_____

_____

_____

_____

_____

_____

_____

_____

_____

_____

His Memories of the First Time We Met

This is the first thing I remember her saying to me...

_____

_____

_____

_____

And this is what I remember us talking about...

_____

_____

_____

Other details I remember about that moment include (examples to include could be a song that was playing, the weather, or who you were with)...

_____

_____

_____

_____

_____

Our First Date...

The day we had our first date was...

_____

The date started at this time...

_____

And this is when it ended...

_____

The person who planned the date was...

_____

This is who talked the most during the date...

_____

_____

This is what she wore...

_____

_____

And this is what he wore...

_____

_____

_____

Our First Date...

And this is what we did...

_____

_____

_____

_____

_____

_____

_____

_____

_____

_____

_____

_____

Getting Serious...

The person who said "I love you" first was...

_____

_____

When they said "I love you" that first time, it was...

☐ Planned.

☐ Spontaneous.

After they had said it, they felt...

_____

_____

_____

_____

(For the other person):
When they told me that they were in love with me, my initial feelings were...

_____

_____

_____

_____

_____

And my response to them was...

_____

_____

_____

_____

And it took me this long to say "I love you" to them...

_____

_____

We first talked about marriage after we had been together this long...

_____

_____

And this is who brought it up first...

_____

_____

We dated this long before we got engaged...

_____

_____

_____

Getting Engaged...

We became engaged on this date...

_____

And this is where we were...

_____

_____

_____

_____

This is what we had been doing before the question was "popped"...

_____

_____

_____

_____

_____

_____

_____

Getting Engaged...

The story of our marriage proposal is...

_____

_____

_____

_____

_____

_____

_____

_____

_____

_____

_____

Her Memories of Getting Engaged

The first person I told was...

_____

_____

_____

This was their reaction...

_____

_____

_____

_____

_____

_____

_____

_____

_____

_____

Her Memories of Getting Engaged

When I think back to the day we got engaged, these are the memories that come to me (things to write about could include where you were, what you were wearing, the weather, any music that was being played, and who you were with)...

_____

_____

_____

_____

_____

_____

_____

_____

_____

_____

_____

His Memories of Getting Engaged

The first person I told was...

_____

_____

This was their reaction...

_____

_____

_____

_____

_____

_____

_____

_____

_____

_____

His Memories of Getting Engaged

When I think back to the day we got engaged, these are the memories that come to me (things to write about could include where you were, what you were wearing, the weather, any music that was being played, and who you were with)...

_____

_____

_____

_____

_____

_____

_____

_____

_____

_____

_____

Our Wedding Day...

If we had to summarize our wedding day into one sentence, it would be...

_____

_____

_____

_____

_____

We were married on this date...

_____

And we were married in this city and place...

_____

_____

The weather that day was...

_____

_____

This is how many guests attended the ceremony...

_____

_____

_____

Our Wedding Day...

This is who was in our wedding party...

_____

_____

_____

_____

_____

_____

_____

_____

_____

_____

_____

_____

Our Wedding Day...

The groomsmen wore...

_____

_____

_____

_____

And the bridesmaids wore...

_____

_____

_____

_____

This is where our ceremony took place...

_____

_____

And the reception was held here...

_____

_____

Getting Married...

These are the wedding day stories and details that have been remembered and talked about for years....

_____

_____

_____

_____

_____

_____

_____

_____

_____

_____

_____

_____

Her Wedding Day Memories

This is what I did and who I was with the night before my wedding day...

_____

_____

_____

_____

_____

_____

_____

_____

_____

_____

_____

_____

Her Wedding Day Memories

And this is what I did and who I was with during the hours leading up to the ceremony...

_____

_____

_____

_____

_____

_____

This is who helped me get ready...

_____

_____

_____

_____

_____

Her Wedding Day Memories

This is how I remember feeling when I first saw myself in the mirror wearing my wedding dress/wedding outfit and about to walk down the aisle...

_____

_____

_____

_____

_____

_____

These are my memories of my wedding dress/wedding outfit....

_____

_____

_____

_____

_____

_____

Her Wedding Day Memories

"Something Olde, Something New, Something Borrowed,
Something Blue, A Sixpence in your Shoe."

According to a Victorian era rhyme, it is good luck for a bride to carry or to include four objects somewhere on her wedding outfit. This tradition, minus the sixpence in the shoe, has continued for many brides.

My "something old" item was...

_____

_____

My "something new" item was...

_____

_____

My "something borrowed" item was...

_____

_____

And my "something blue" item was...

_____

_____

I was walked down the aisle by...

_____

_____

_____

Her Wedding Day Memories

When I close my eyes and think about those moments right before we were married, I remember...

Feeling these emotions...

_____

_____

_____

_____

Thinking this as I looked across at my about-to-be-husband...

_____

_____

_____

_____

And noticing these things...

_____

_____

_____

_____

Her Wedding Day Memories

This is how I remember him looking and what he was wearing...

_____

_____

_____

_____

_____

_____

_____

This is what I remember thinking in the immediate moments after being officially declared "husband and wife"...

_____

_____

_____

_____

_____

His Wedding Day Memories

This is what I did and who I was with the night before my wedding day...

_____

_____

_____

_____

_____

_____

_____

_____

_____

_____

_____

His Wedding Day Memories

And this is what I did and who I was with during the hours leading up to the ceremony...

_____

_____

_____

_____

_____

_____

_____

This is who helped me get ready...

_____

_____

_____

_____

_____

His Wedding Day Memories

This is how I remember feeling when I first saw myself in the mirror wearing my wedding clothes and about to walk down the aisle...

_____

_____

_____

_____

_____

These are my memories of what I was wearing....

_____

_____

_____

_____

_____

_____

His Wedding Day Memories

When I close my eyes and think about those moments right before we were married, I remember...

Feeling these emotions...

_____

_____

_____

_____

Thinking this as I looked across at my about-to-be-wife...

_____

_____

_____

And noticing these things...

_____

_____

_____

_____

This is how I remember her looking and what she was wearing...

_____

_____

_____

_____

_____

_____

_____

_____

_____

_____

His Wedding Day Memories

This is what I remember thinking in the immediate moments after being officially declared "husband and wife"...

_____

_____

_____

_____

_____

_____

_____

_____

_____

_____

_____

Wedding Reception/What We Did Next

After the wedding ceremony, we...

☐ Had a traditional wedding reception.

☐ Had a small gathering of close friends and family.

☐ Spent the day/evening just the two of us.

☐ Other: _____

_____

_____

_____

(If you had a traditional wedding reception):

Our wedding reception was held here...

_____

_____

We had this many guests in attendance...

_____

The menu was...

_____

_____

_____

_____

Wedding Reception/What We Did Next

We had our first dance to this song...

_____

_____

Other memories include...

_____

_____

_____

_____

_____

_____

_____

_____

_____

Our Honeymoon/How We Relaxed

After we were married, we...

- ☐ Went on a honeymoon immediately after the wedding.
- ☐ We went on a honeymoon, but it was on a later date.
- ☐ Being married is the best vacation of all!
- ☐ Other: _____

_____

_____

_____

(If you went on a traditional honeymoon):

We went on a trip to...

_____

_____

_____

_____

Our time away lasted this long...

_____

_____

To get there, we traveled by...

_____

_____

Our Honeymoon/How We Relaxed

A few of our favorite honeymoon memories are...

_____

_____

_____

_____

_____

_____

_____

_____

_____

_____

_____

_____

Our First Home Together

Our first home we lived in after we were married was...

_____

_____

It had this many bedrooms and bathrooms...

_____

_____

And it cost us this much each month to live there...

_____

_____

We chose this place because...

_____

_____

_____

_____

_____

_____

Our First Home Together

The neighborhood where it was located is best described this way...

_____

_____

_____

_____

Our neighbors were...

_____

_____

_____

_____

_____

We lived here this long...

_____

_____

Her First Home Memories

When I think about our first home, these are the memories that come to mind...

_____

_____

_____

_____

_____

_____

_____

_____

_____

_____

_____

_____

His First Home Memories

When I think about our first home, these are the memories that come to mind...

_____

_____

_____

_____

_____

_____

_____

_____

_____

_____

_____

"Babies are such a nice way to start people."

– Don Herold

Grandparents Begin as Babies

Grandmothers Begin as Babies

My birthdate is...

_____

The city I was born in was...

_____

And the place I was born was (hospital, at home, another place)...

_____

My full name at birth was...

_____

This name was selected because...

_____

_____

_____

I was this length and weight when I was born...

_____

My first words were...

_____

_____

I took my first steps at age...

_____

Grandfathers Begin as Babies

My birthdate is...

_____

The city I was born in was...

_____

And the place I was born was (hospital, at home, another place)...

_____

My full name at birth was...

_____

This name was selected because...

_____

_____

I was this length and weight when I was born...

_____

My first words were...

_____

_____

I took my first steps at age...

_____

Grandmothers Begin as Babies

My parents were this age when they had me...

_____

_____

The stories I have been told about the day I was born are...

_____

_____

_____

_____

_____

_____

_____

_____

Grandfathers Begin as Babies

My parents were this age when they had me...

_____

_____

The stories I have been told about the day I was born are...

_____

_____

_____

_____

_____

_____

_____

_____

Grandmothers Begin as Babies

This is what I have been told I was like when I was a baby...

_____

_____

_____

_____

_____

_____

_____

_____

_____

_____

_____

_____

Grandfathers Begin as Babies

This is what I have been told I was like when I was a baby...

_____

_____

_____

_____

_____

_____

_____

_____

_____

_____

_____

Grandmothers Begin as Babies

According to those who know, I really loved these songs when I was a baby...

_____

_____

_____

_____

And these toys...

_____

_____

_____

_____

And these books...

_____

_____

_____

_____

Grandfathers Begin as Babies

According to those who know, I really loved these songs when I was a baby...

_____

_____

_____

_____

And these toys...

_____

_____

_____

_____

And these books...

_____

_____

_____

_____

If You Were Adopted: Her Memories

I was this age when I was adopted...

_____

And I was this age when I found out that I had been adopted...

_____

I was told by...

_____

_____

The story of me being told about my adoption is...

_____

_____

_____

_____

_____

_____

If You Were Adopted: His Memories

I was this age when I was adopted...

_____

And I was this age when I found out that I had been adopted...

_____

I was told by...

_____

_____

The story of me being told about my adoption is...

_____

_____

_____

_____

_____

_____

_____

This is what I know about my birth parents...

_____

_____

_____

_____

_____

_____

After all these years, I still have these questions about my birth parents
and my being adopted...

_____

_____

_____

_____

_____

_____

If You Were Adopted: His Memories

This is what I know about my birth parents...

_____

_____

_____

_____

_____

_____

After all these years, I still have these questions about my birth parents
and my being adopted...

_____

_____

_____

_____

_____

_____

What Happened the Year She Was Born?

(Google the following for the year you were born.)

Notable and historical events that occurred the year I was born include...

_____

_____

_____

_____

The movie that won the Academy Award for Best Picture...

_____

_____

Best actress...

_____

Best actor...

_____

A few popular movies that came out the year I was born...

_____

_____

_____

_____

What Happened the Year She Was Born?

A few songs that were on the top of the music charts...

_____

_____

_____

_____

Famous people who were born the same month and year I was...

_____

_____

_____

_____

The prices of the following items were...

- A loaf of bread: _____

- A gallon of milk: _____

- A cup of coffee: _____

- The average cost of a new home: _____

- A first-class stamp: _____

- A gallon of gas: _____

- A movie ticket: _____

What Happened the Year He Was Born?

(Google the following for the year you were born.)

Notable and historical events that occurred the year I was born include...

_____

_____

_____

_____

The movie that won the Academy Award for Best Picture...

_____

_____

Best actress...

_____

Best actor...

_____

A few popular movies that came out the year I was born...

_____

_____

_____

_____

What Happened the Year He Was Born?

A few songs that were on the top of the music charts...

_____

_____

_____

_____

Famous people who were born the same month and year I was...

_____

_____

_____

_____

The prices of the following items were...

- A loaf of bread: _____

- A gallon of milk: _____

- A cup of coffee: _____

- The average cost of a new home: _____

- A first-class stamp: _____

- A gallon of gas: _____

- A movie ticket: _____

"At some point
in your childhood,
you and your
friends
went outside
to play together for
the last time,
and nobody
knew it."
– Author Unknown

Growing Up

Her Memories of Her Childhood

When I was a kid, most people called me...

_____

But sometimes they would use this nickname...

_____

I was given that nickname because...

_____

_____

_____

I would describe myself when I was a kid this way...

_____

_____

_____

_____

...and my childhood this way...

_____

_____

_____

_____

His Memories of His Childhood

When I was a kid, most people called me...

_____

But sometimes they would use this nickname...

_____

I was given that nickname because...

_____

_____

_____

I would describe myself when I was a kid this way...

_____

_____

_____

_____

...and my childhood this way...

_____

_____

_____

_____

Her Memories of Her Childhood

When I was a kid, I remember playing these games...

_____

_____

_____

And cherishing these toys...

_____

_____

_____

_____

And loving these television shows...

_____

_____

_____

_____

His Memories of His Childhood

When I was a kid, I remember playing these games...

_____

_____

_____

And cherishing these toys...

_____

_____

_____

_____

And loving these television shows...

_____

_____

_____

_____

_____

Her Memories of Her Childhood

When I was a kid, I remember loving these movies...

_____

_____

_____

_____

And these songs...

_____

_____

_____

_____

And these books...

_____

_____

_____

_____

_____

His Memories of His Childhood

When I was a kid, I remember loving these movies...

_____

_____

_____

_____

And these songs...

_____

_____

_____

_____

And these books...

_____

_____

_____

_____

Her Memories of Her Childhood

During my elementary school years, my best friends were...

_____

_____

_____

_____

The last time I communicated with them was...

_____

_____

_____

_____

The elementary school teacher that I most fondly remember is...

_____

_____

The thing I most remember about them is...

_____

_____

_____

_____

His Memories of His Childhood

During my elementary school years, my best friends were...

_____

_____

_____

_____

The last time I communicated with them was...

_____

_____

_____

_____

The elementary school teacher that I most fondly remember is...

_____

_____

The thing I most remember about them is...

_____

_____

_____

_____

Her Memories of Her Childhood

My regular chores when I was kid included...

_____

_____

_____

_____

In return I received an allowance of...

_____

_____

When I had money, I would typically spend it on...

_____

_____

_____

When I was a kid, I dreamed of becoming a...

_____

_____

_____

His Memories of His Childhood

My regular chores when I was kid included...

_____

_____

_____

_____

In return I received an allowance of...

_____

_____

When I had money, I would typically spend it on...

_____

_____

_____

When I was a kid, I dreamed of becoming a...

_____

_____

_____

If I could be a kid again for just one day, I would...

_____

_____

_____

_____

_____

_____

_____

_____

_____

_____

_____

His Memories of His Childhood

If I could be a kid again for just one day, I would...

_____

_____

_____

_____

_____

_____

_____

_____

_____

_____

_____

Her Memories of Her Childhood

One of my favorite childhood memories is...

_____

_____

_____

_____

_____

_____

_____

_____

_____

_____

His Memories of His Childhood

One of my favorite childhood memories is...

_____

_____

_____

_____

_____

_____

_____

_____

_____

_____

_____

Her Memories of Her Childhood

This is where we lived during my elementary and junior high school years...

_____

_____

_____

This is how I would describe where we lived during this period of my life...

_____

_____

_____

_____

_____

During the years of my childhood, I spent my summers doing...

_____

_____

_____

_____

_____

His Memories of His Childhood

This is where we lived during my elementary and junior high school years...

_____

_____

_____

This is how I would describe where we lived during this period of my life...

_____

_____

_____

_____

_____

During the years of my childhood, I spent my summers doing...

_____

_____

_____

_____

Her Memories of Her Childhood

It is common for kids to have an attachment to an object such as a specific blanket or toy or stuffed animal. For me, that item was...

_____

_____

The name I had for this item was...

_____

The story of how this special item came into my life is...

_____

_____

_____

When I close my eyes and think about this important part of me and my childhood, I feel...

_____

_____

_____

_____

His Memories of His Childhood

It is common for kids to have an attachment to an object such as a specific blanket or toy or stuffed animal. For me, that item was...

_____

_____

The name I had for this item was...

_____

The story of how this special item came into my life is...

_____

_____

_____

When I close my eyes and think about this important part of me and my childhood, I feel...

_____

_____

_____

_____

_____

Her Memories: This is How I Remember My Childhood Bedroom...

The walls were this color...

_____

My bedding looked like this...

_____

_____

I had these things on the walls...

_____

_____

_____

Additional important details about my childhood bedroom include...

_____

_____

_____

_____

_____

_____

His Memories: This is How I Remember
My Childhood Bedroom...

The walls were this color...

_____

My bedding looked like this...

_____

_____

I had these things on the walls...

_____

_____

_____

Additional important details about my childhood bedroom include...

_____

_____

_____

_____

_____

_____

Family Memories
From When She was Growing Up

We ate dinner together this number of times each week...

_____

_____

When we did eat together, the meal typically followed this routine...

_____

_____

_____

_____

_____

The person who usually cooked was...

_____

_____

And the clean up afterwards was usually done by...

_____

_____

Family Memories
From When He was Growing Up

We ate dinner together this number of times each week...

_____

_____

When we did eat together, the meal typically followed this routine...

_____

_____

_____

_____

_____

The person who usually cooked was...

_____

_____

And the clean up afterwards was usually done by...

_____

_____

Family Memories
From When She was Growing Up

A recipe, dish, or food item that reminds me of my childhood is...

_____

_____

_____

Specifically, when I think of this dish, I remember...

_____

_____

_____

_____

_____

The family recipes I would love to eat again are...

_____

_____

_____

_____

Family Memories
From When He was Growing Up

A recipe, dish, or food item that reminds me of my childhood is...

_____

_____

_____

Specifically, when I think of this dish, I remember...

_____

_____

_____

_____

The family recipes I would love to eat again are...

_____

_____

_____

_____

Family Memories
From When She was Growing Up

The holiday that was the biggest deal in our family was...

_____

_____

_____

We would celebrate this holiday by...

_____

_____

_____

_____

_____

_____

_____

_____

Family Memories
From When He was Growing Up

The holiday that was the biggest deal in our family was...

_____

_____

_____

We would celebrate this holiday by...

_____

_____

_____

_____

_____

_____

_____

_____

Family Memories
From When She was Growing Up

When it comes to religion in my family when I was growing up:

☐ Religion was a big part of my growing up years.

☐ We were religious, but only occasionally attended formal services.

☐ We had our own traditions.

☐ Religion wasn't a part of my early years.

☐ Other: _____

_____

_____

The way that my family's religious traditions and beliefs impacted my current views and religious traditions is...

_____

_____

_____

_____

_____

_____

_____

Family Memories
From When He was Growing Up

When it comes to religion in my family when I was growing up:

☐ Religion was a big part of my growing up years.

☐ We were religious, but only occasionally attended formal services.

☐ We had our own traditions.

☐ Religion wasn't a part of my early years.

☐ Other: _____

_____

_____

The way that my family's religious traditions and beliefs impacted my current views and religious traditions is...

_____

_____

_____

_____

_____

_____

_____

"Teenager:
when you are
too young to
do half the things
you want to do
and too old
for the other half."

– Author Unknown

The Teen Years

Her Memories: When I Was a Teenager...

This is how I would describe myself when I was a teenager...

_____

_____

_____

_____

_____

This is how I dressed and styled my hair in my high school years...

_____

_____

_____

_____

_____

_____

His Memories: When I Was a Teenager...

This is how I would describe myself when I was a teenager...

_____

_____

_____

_____

_____

This is how I dressed and styled my hair in my high school years...

_____

_____

_____

_____

_____

_____

Her Memories: When I Was a Teenager...

During my teenage years, the people I mainly hung out with were...

_____

_____

_____

_____

The last time we talked was...

_____

_____

_____

My parents' opinion of my choice in friends was...

_____

_____

_____

_____

His Memories: When I Was a Teenager...

During my teenage years, the people I mainly hung out with were...

_____

_____

_____

_____

The last time we talked was...

_____

_____

_____

My parents' opinion of my choice in friends was...

_____

_____

_____

_____

Her Memories: When I Was a Teenager...

A typical weekend night during my high school years was spent...

_____

_____

_____

_____

_____

My curfew in high school was...

_____

_____

One memorable time I missed my curfew was because I was...

_____

_____

_____

_____

_____

His Memories: When I Was a Teenager...

A typical weekend night during my high school years was spent...

_____

_____

_____

_____

_____

My curfew in high school was...

_____

_____

One memorable time I missed my curfew was because I was...

_____

_____

_____

_____

_____

Her Memories: When I Was a Teenager...

My parents' response to me missing my curfew was...

_____

_____

_____

_____

I would describe my high school dating life this way...

_____

_____

_____

_____

I got my driver's license when I was this age...

_____

The principal person who taught me how to drive was...

_____

_____

The car I learned to drive in was a (year, make, and model)...

_____

_____

His Memories: When I Was a Teenager...

My parents' response to me missing my curfew was...

_____

_____

_____

_____

I would describe my high school dating life this way...

_____

_____

_____

_____

I got my driver's license when I was this age...

_____

_____

The principal person who taught me how to drive was...

_____

_____

The car I learned to drive in was a (year, make, and model)...

_____

_____

Her Memories: When I Was a Teenager...

The year I graduated from high school was...

_____

My graduating class had this many students in it...

_____

My grades were typically in this range...

_____

_____

My favorite and least favorite subjects were...

_____

_____

_____

The school activities and sports that I participated in were...

_____

_____

_____

_____

_____

His Memories: When I Was a Teenager...

The year I graduated from high school was...

_____

My graduating class had this many students in it...

_____

My grades were typically in this range...

_____

_____

My favorite and least favorite subjects were...

_____

_____

_____

The school activities and sports that I participated in were...

_____

_____

_____

_____

_____

The things I liked about high school were...

_____

_____

_____

_____

_____

_____

...and these are the things I disliked...

_____

_____

_____

_____

_____

_____

_____

His Memories: When I Was a Teenager...

The things I liked about high school were...

_____

_____

_____

_____

_____

...and these are the things I disliked...

_____

_____

_____

_____

_____

I loved these bands/musicians...

_____

_____

_____

_____

And these songs...

_____

_____

_____

_____

And these movies...

_____

_____

_____

_____

His Memories: When I Was a Teenager...

I loved these bands/musicians...

_____

_____

_____

And these songs...

_____

_____

_____

And these movies...

_____

_____

_____

When I was a teenager...

And these television shows...

_____

_____

_____

_____

And these books...

_____

_____

_____

_____

And doing these activities...

_____

_____

_____

_____

When I was a teenager...

And these television shows...

_____

_____

_____

_____

And these books...

_____

_____

_____

_____

And doing these activities...

_____

_____

_____

_____

Her Memories: When I Was a Teenager...

During my high school years, we lived here...

_____

_____

_____

I would describe where we lived this way...

_____

_____

_____

_____

_____

_____

_____

_____

_____

His Memories: When I Was a Teenager...

During my high school years, we lived here...

_____

_____

_____

I would describe where we lived this way...

_____

_____

_____

_____

_____

_____

_____

_____

Her Memories: This is How I Remember My Teenage Bedroom...

The walls were this color...

_____

My bedding looked like this...

_____

_____

I had these things on the walls...

_____

_____

_____

And my favorite place to hide things was...

_____

Additional important details include...

_____

_____

_____

_____

_____

His Memories: This is How I Remember My Teenage Bedroom...

The walls were this color...

_____

My bedding looked like this...

_____

_____

I had these things on the walls...

_____

_____

_____

And my favorite place to hide things was...

_____

Additional important details include...

_____

_____

_____

_____

Her Memories: When I Was a Teenager...

Knowing what I know now, the advice I would give my teenage self is...

Knowing what I know now, the advice I would give my teenage self is...

_____

_____

_____

_____

_____

_____

_____

_____

_____

_____

_____

A teacher, coach, or mentor who had a huge impact on me becoming who I am today is...

_____

_____

The specific influences they had on me and my life were...

_____

_____

_____

_____

_____

_____

_____

_____

_____

_____

His Memories: When I Was a Teenager...

A teacher, coach, or mentor who had a huge impact on me becoming who I am today is...

_____

_____

The specific influences they had on me and my life were...

_____

_____

_____

_____

_____

_____

_____

_____

"Love
doesn't make
the world go
round.
Love
is what makes
the ride
worthwhile."
– Franklin P. Jones

Relationships

Thoughts on Relationships

The most important factors that keep a relationship strong and healthy are...

_____

_____

_____

_____

_____

_____

_____

_____

_____

_____

_____

Thoughts on Relationships

Looking at our relationship, the main reasons we think we have endured and thrived this long are...

_____

_____

_____

_____

_____

_____

_____

_____

_____

_____

_____

Knowing all I know now, the advice I would give myself when we first got married is...

_____

_____

_____

_____

_____

_____

_____

_____

_____

_____

_____

_____

His Thoughts on Relationships

Knowing all I know now, the advice I would give myself when we first got married is...

_____

_____

_____

_____

_____

_____

_____

_____

_____

_____

_____

"Adulthood is like a dog going to the vet; we're all excited for the car ride until we realize where we're actually going."

– Author Unknown

Becoming an Adult

Her Memories on Starting Adulthood

After high school I made the decision to...

- ☐ Start college.
- ☐ Join the military.
- ☐ Get a job.
- ☐ Take a break.
- ☐ Other: _____

I made this decision because...

_____

_____

_____

_____

_____

_____

_____

Looking back, this is how I now feel about my decision...

- ☐ It was the right one, at the right time.
- ☐ It was the right direction to go in, but the wrong time to do it.
- ☐ You can't get them all right.
- ☐ The jury's still out.

His Memories on Starting Adulthood

After high school I made the decision to...

□ Start college.

□ Join the military.

□ Get a job.

□ Take a break.

□ Other: _____

I made this decision because...

_____

_____

_____

_____

_____

_____

_____

Looking back, this is how I now feel about my decision...

□ It was the right one, at the right time.

□ It was the right direction to go in, but the wrong time to do it.

□ You can't get them all right.

□ The jury's still out.

Her Memories on Starting Adulthood

I think that this was the correct or incorrect decision because...

_____

_____

_____

_____

_____

_____

This period impacted my life in this way...

_____

_____

_____

_____

_____

_____

I think that this was the correct or incorrect decision because...

_____

_____

_____

_____

_____

This period impacted my life in this way...

_____

_____

_____

_____

_____

Her Memories on Starting Adulthood

I got my first job when I was this age...

_____

The job was...

_____

_____

...and I was paid this much...

_____

So far, the total number of jobs I have had in my lifetime is...

_____

The first job I ever quit was...

_____

A few of my favorite jobs were...

_____

_____

...and my least favorites...

_____

_____

His Memories on Starting Adulthood

I got my first job when I was this age...

_____

The job was...

_____

_____

...and I was paid this much...

_____

So far, the total number of jobs I have had in my lifetime is...

_____

The first job I ever quit was...

_____

A few of my favorite jobs were...

_____

_____

...and my least favorites...

_____

_____

These are the places where I have lived during my life; I have included when I lived in each one...

_____

_____

_____

_____

_____

_____

_____

_____

_____

_____

_____

His Memories on Starting Adulthood

These are the places where I have lived during my life; I have included when I lived in each one...

_____

_____

_____

_____

_____

_____

_____

_____

_____

_____

_____

"It's better
to be
an optimist
who is
sometimes wrong
than
a pessimist
who is
always right."
– Mark Twain

More About Us

More About Her

If I were to write an autobiography, the title would be...

_____

_____

_____

One of my favorite quotes is...

_____

_____

_____

The central values I have tried to live my life by are...

_____

_____

_____

_____

_____

_____

More About Him

If I were to write an autobiography, the title would be...

_____

_____

_____

One of my favorite quotes is...

_____

_____

_____

The central values I have tried to live my life by are...

_____

_____

_____

_____

_____

More About Her

I am who I am today in large part because of these experiences...

_____

_____

_____

_____

_____

_____

_____

_____

_____

_____

_____

More About Him

I am who I am today in large part because of these experiences...

_____

_____

_____

_____

_____

_____

_____

_____

_____

_____

_____

And I am who I am today in large part because of these people...

_____

_____

_____

_____

_____

_____

_____

_____

_____

_____

_____

More About Him

And I am who I am today in large part because of these people...

_____

_____

_____

_____

_____

_____

_____

_____

_____

_____

_____

A few of my proudest personal accomplishments are...

_____

_____

_____

_____

_____

_____

_____

_____

_____

_____

A few of my proudest personal accomplishments are...

_____

_____

_____

_____

_____

_____

_____

_____

_____

_____

_____

More About Her

The hardest thing I have had to overcome in my life is...

_____

_____

_____

_____

_____

I succeeded in overcoming this challenge because of these decisions, actions, and people...

_____

_____

_____

_____

_____

_____

More About Him

The hardest thing I have had to overcome in my life is...

_____

_____

_____

_____

_____

I succeeded in overcoming this challenge because of these decisions, actions, and people...

_____

_____

_____

_____

_____

_____

More About Her

This is how I hope to be remembered...

_____

_____

_____

_____

_____

_____

_____

_____

_____

_____

More About Him

This is how I hope to be remembered...

_____

_____

_____

_____

_____

_____

_____

_____

_____

_____

_____

"We never know the love of a parent till we become parents ourselves."

– Henry Ward Beecher

Her Memories of Her Parents

My mother's full name is...

_____

...and her maiden name is...

_____

This is where she was born...

_____

...and where she grew up...

_____

_____

_____

Her family was from this/these part(s) of the world...

_____

_____

Her highest level of schooling was...

_____

And her occupations were...

_____

_____

_____

Her Memories of Her Parents

The way I would describe my mother is...

_____

_____

_____

_____

_____

_____

_____

_____

She was good at many things, but was especially talented and skilled at...

_____

_____

_____

_____

Her Memories of Her Parents

My mom and I are alike in these ways...

_____

_____

_____

_____

_____

_____

And this is how we are different...

_____

_____

_____

_____

_____

_____

Her Memories of Her Parents

I would describe our relationship when I was a kid this way...

_____

_____

_____

_____

...and this way during my teens...

_____

_____

_____

_____

...and in my later years...

_____

_____

_____

_____

One of my favorite memories of my mother is...

_____

_____

_____

_____

_____

_____

_____

_____

_____

_____

Her Memories of Her Parents

Some of the best advice she gave me was...

_____

_____

_____

_____

_____

_____

_____

_____

_____

_____

_____

Her Memories of Her Parents

My father's full name is...

_____

His mother's maiden name is...

_____

This is where he was born...

_____

...and where he grew up...

_____

_____

His family was from this/these part(s) of the world...

_____

_____

His highest level of schooling was...

_____

And his occupations were...

_____

_____

_____

The way I would describe my father is...

_____

_____

_____

_____

_____

_____

_____

He was good at many things, but was especially talented and skilled at...

_____

_____

_____

_____

My father and I are alike in these ways...

_____

_____

_____

_____

_____

_____

And this is how we are different...

_____

_____

_____

_____

_____

_____

Her Memories of Her Parents

I would describe our relationship when I was a kid this way...

_____

_____

_____

_____

...and this way during my teens...

_____

_____

_____

...and in my later years...

_____

_____

_____

One of my favorite memories of my father is...

_____

_____

_____

_____

_____

_____

_____

_____

_____

_____

_____

Some of the best advice he gave me was...

_____

_____

_____

_____

_____

_____

_____

_____

_____

_____

Her Memories of Her Parents

My parents were married on this date...

_____

Their ages when they were married were...

_____

_____

The story of the way my parents met is...

_____

_____

_____

_____

_____

_____

_____

_____

Her Memories of Her Parents

A list of people other than my parents who helped raise me includes...

_____

_____

_____

_____

_____

_____

_____

_____

_____

_____

"There is
no friendship,
no love,
like that
of the parent
for the child."

– Henry Ward Beecher

His Memories
of His Parents

His Memories of His Parents

My mother's full name is...

_____

...and her maiden name is...

_____

This is where she was born...

_____

...and where she grew up...

_____

_____

_____

Her family was from this/these part(s) of the world...

_____

_____

Her highest level of schooling was...

_____

And her occupations were...

_____

_____

_____

The way I would describe my mother is...

_____

_____

_____

_____

_____

_____

_____

She was good at many things, but was especially talented and skilled at...

_____

_____

_____

_____

His Memories of His Parents

My mom and I are alike in these ways...

_____

_____

_____

_____

_____

_____

And this is how we are different...

_____

_____

_____

_____

_____

_____

His Memories of His Parents

I would describe our relationship when I was a kid this way...

_____

_____

_____

_____

...and this way during my teens...

_____

_____

_____

_____

...and in my later years...

_____

_____

_____

_____

His Memories of His Parents

One of my favorite memories of my mother is...

_____

_____

_____

_____

_____

_____

_____

_____

_____

_____

_____

His Memories of His Parents

Some of the best advice she gave me was...

_____

_____

_____

_____

_____

_____

_____

_____

_____

_____

_____

His Memories of His Parents

My father's full name is...

_____

His mother's maiden name is...

_____

This is where he was born...

_____

...and where he grew up...

_____

_____

His family was from this/these part(s) of the world...

_____

_____

His highest level of schooling was...

_____

And his occupations were...

_____

_____

_____

His Memories of His Parents

The way I would describe my father is...

_____

_____

_____

_____

_____

_____

_____

He was good at many things, but was especially talented and skilled at...

_____

_____

_____

_____

His Memories of His Parents

My father and I are alike in these ways...

_____

_____

_____

_____

_____

_____

And this is how we are different...

_____

_____

_____

_____

_____

His Memories of His Parents

I would describe our relationship when I was a kid this way...

_____

_____

_____

_____

...and this way during my teens...

_____

_____

_____

...and in my later years...

_____

_____

_____

His Memories of His Parents

One of my favorite memories of my father is...

_____

_____

_____

_____

_____

_____

_____

_____

_____

_____

_____

_____

His Memories of His Parents

Some of the best advice he gave me was...

_____

_____

_____

_____

_____

_____

_____

_____

_____

_____

His Memories of His Parents

My parents were married on this date...

_____

Their ages when they were married were...

_____

_____

The story of the way my parents met is...

_____

_____

_____

_____

_____

_____

_____

_____

His Memories of His Parents

A list of people other than my parents who helped raise me includes...

\
\
\
\
\
\
\
\
\
\
\

"The best things in life and about life aren't things."

– Author Unknown

Favorite Things

Her Favorite Things

My favorite color is...

_____

My favorite season of the year is...

_____

My favorite holiday is...

_____

_____

My favorite decade for music is...

_____

_____

_____

And my favorite music genre is...

_____

_____

_____

The movie I have watched the greatest number of times is...

_____

_____

His Favorite Things

My favorite color is...

_____

My favorite season of the year is...

_____

My favorite holiday is...

_____

_____

My favorite decade for music is...

_____

_____

_____

And my favorite music genre is...

_____

_____

_____

The movie I have watched the greatest number of times is...

_____

_____

Her Favorite Things

A few of my favorite places I have traveled to are...

_____

_____

_____

_____

_____

_____

_____

_____

_____

_____

_____

His Favorite Things

A few of my favorite places I have traveled to are...

_____

_____

_____

_____

_____

_____

_____

_____

_____

_____

_____

My favorite travel memory is...

_____

_____

_____

_____

_____

_____

_____

_____

_____

_____

_____

_____

His Favorite Things

My favorite travel memory is...

Her Favorite Things

The books that have majorly impacted the way I think, work, or live my life are...

1. _____

2. _____

3. _____

4. _____

5. _____

6. _____

7. _____

8. _____

9. _____

10. _____

11. _____

12. _____

13. _____

14. _____

15. _____

His Favorite Things

The books that have majorly impacted the way I think, work, or live my life are...

1. _____

2. _____

3. _____

4. _____

5. _____

6. _____

7. _____

8. _____

9. _____

10. _____

11. _____

12. _____

13. _____

14. _____

15. _____

Her Favorite Things

My top ten favorite television shows of all time...

1. _____

2. _____

3. _____

4. _____

5. _____

6. _____

7. _____

8. _____

9. _____

10. _____

His Favorite Things

My top ten favorite television shows of all time...

1. _____

2. _____

3. _____

4. _____

5. _____

6. _____

7. _____

8. _____

9. _____

10. _____

Her Favorite Things

My top ten favorite movies of all time...

1. _____

2. _____

3. _____

4. _____

5. _____

6. _____

7. _____

8. _____

9. _____

10. _____

His Favorite Things

My top ten favorite movies of all time...

1. _____

2. _____

3. _____

4. _____

5. _____

6. _____

7. _____

8. _____

9. _____

10. _____

Her Favorite Things

If I were to create a playlist of my favorite music throughout my life, it would include these songs and musical compositions:

1. _____

2. _____

3. _____

4. _____

5. _____

6. _____

7. _____

8. _____

9. _____

10. _____

11. _____

12. _____

13. _____

14. _____

15. _____

His Favorite Things

If I were to create a playlist of my favorite music throughout my life, it would include these songs and musical compositions:

1. _____

2. _____

3. _____

4. _____

5. _____

6. _____

7. _____

8. _____

9. _____

10. _____

11. _____

12. _____

13. _____

14. _____

15. _____

"Grandparents are a little bit parent, a little bit teacher, and a little bit best friend."

– Author Unknown

Our Grandparents

Her Memories of Her Grandparents

My grandparents' names on my mother's side are...

_____

_____

My maternal grandmother's maiden name was...

_____

I called them...

_____

This is when and where they were born and where they grew up...

_____

_____

_____

Their highest level of schooling was...

_____

_____

Their occupations were...

_____

_____

_____

Her Memories of Her Grandparents

I would describe my grandparents on my mother's side this way...

_____

_____

_____

_____

_____

_____

_____

_____

_____

_____

Her Memories of Her Grandparents

My grandparents' names on my father's side are...

_____

_____

My paternal grandmother's maiden name was...

_____

I called them...

_____

This is when and where they were born and where they grew up...

_____

_____

_____

Their highest level of schooling was...

_____

_____

Their occupations were...

_____

_____

_____

Her Memories of Her Grandparents

I would describe my grandparents on my father's side this way...

_____

_____

_____

_____

_____

_____

_____

_____

_____

_____

His Memories of His Grandparents

My grandparents' names on my mother's side are...

_____

_____

My maternal grandmother's maiden name was...

_____

I called them...

_____

This is when and where they were born and where they grew up...

_____

_____

_____

Their highest level of schooling was...

_____

_____

Their occupations were...

_____

_____

_____

His Memories of His Grandparents

I would describe my grandparents on my mother's side this way...

_____

_____

_____

_____

_____

_____

_____

_____

_____

_____

His Memories of His Grandparents

My grandparents' names on my father's side are...

_____

_____

My paternal grandmother's maiden name was...

_____

I called them...

_____

This is when and where they were born and where they grew up...

_____

_____

_____

Their highest level of schooling was...

_____

_____

Their occupations were...

_____

_____

_____

His Memories of His Grandparents

I would describe my grandparents on my father's side this way...

_____

_____

_____

_____

_____

_____

_____

_____

_____

_____

_____

"A perfect marriage is two imperfect people who refuse to give up on each other."

– Author Unknown

More About Us

If I could have dinner with any five people who have ever lived, I would invite...

_____

_____

_____

_____

So far, the ten-year period of my life that I most fondly look back on is...

_____

_____

I think I remember this time so warmly because...

_____

_____

_____

_____

_____

More About Him

If I could have dinner with any five people who have ever lived, I would invite...

_____

_____

_____

_____

So far, the ten-year period of my life that I most fondly look back on is...

_____

_____

I think I remember this time so warmly because...

_____

_____

_____

_____

_____

More About Her

My longest friendship has been with...

_____

_____

I have known them since...

_____

_____

The story of how we met is...

_____

_____

_____

_____

_____

If I could live anywhere in the world for a year with all expenses paid, I would choose to live here...

_____

_____

_____

More About Him

My longest friendship has been with...

_____

_____

I have known them since...

_____

_____

The story of how we met is...

_____

_____

_____

_____

_____

If I could live anywhere in the world for a year with all expenses paid, I would choose to live here...

_____

_____

_____

More About Her

I identify myself politically this way...

_____

The main ways my political views have changed over the course of my life are...

_____

_____

_____

If I woke up tomorrow to find myself in charge of the country, the first three things I would enact or change are...

1. _____

   _____

2. _____

   _____

3. _____

   _____

More About Him

I identify myself politically this way...

_____

_____

The main ways my political views have changed over the course of my life are...

_____

_____

_____

_____

If I woke up tomorrow to find myself in charge of the country, the first three things I would enact or change are...

4. _____

_____

5. _____

_____

6. _____

_____

The religious and spiritual practices that are a part of my daily life are...

_____

_____

_____

_____

_____

The ways my spiritual and religious practices have changed and evolved over the course of my life are...

_____

_____

_____

_____

_____

_____

More About Him

The religious and spiritual practices that are a part of my daily life are...

_____

_____

_____

_____

_____

The ways my spiritual and religious practices have changed and evolved over the course of my life are...

_____

_____

_____

_____

_____

_____

More About Her

If I had to choose between fate or free will, I believe this one has the biggest impact on our lives:

_____

A miracle I have personally experienced is...

_____

_____

_____

_____

_____

When times are tough, this is how I give myself the inner-strength I need...

_____

_____

_____

_____

_____

_____

More About Him

If I had to choose between fate or free will, I believe this one has the biggest impact on our lives:

_____

A miracle I have personally experienced is...

_____

_____

_____

_____

_____

When times are tough, this is how I give myself the inner-strength I need...

_____

_____

_____

_____

_____

_____

"Sibling:
a combination
of a best friend
and a pain
in the neck."

– Author Unknown

Brothers & Sisters

Her Memories of Her Siblings

I have this many brothers and sisters...

_____

I am the oldest/middle/youngest or only child...

_____

My siblings' names and birthdates are...

_____

_____

_____

_____

_____

_____

_____

_____

_____

Her Memories of Her Siblings

One of my favorite memories of one or more of my siblings is...

_____

_____

_____

_____

_____

_____

_____

_____

_____

_____

_____

Her Memories of Her Siblings

Another favorite memory of one or more of my siblings is...

_____

_____

_____

_____

_____

_____

_____

_____

_____

_____

Another favorite memory of one or more of my siblings is...

_____

_____

_____

_____

_____

_____

_____

_____

_____

_____

_____

_____

Another favorite memory of one or more of my siblings is...

_____

_____

_____

_____

_____

_____

_____

_____

_____

_____

_____

_____

Her Memories of Her Siblings

Another favorite memory of one or more of my siblings is...

_____

_____

_____

_____

_____

_____

_____

_____

_____

_____

_____

His Memories of His Siblings

I have this many brothers and sisters...

_____

I am the oldest/middle/youngest or only child...

_____

My siblings' names and birthdates are...

_____

_____

_____

_____

_____

_____

_____

_____

_____

His Memories of His Siblings

One of my favorite memories of one or more of my siblings is...

_____

_____

_____

_____

_____

_____

_____

_____

_____

_____

_____

His Memories of His Siblings

Another favorite memory of one or more of my siblings is...

_____

_____

_____

_____

_____

_____

_____

_____

_____

_____

_____

His Memories of His Siblings

Another favorite memory of one or more of my siblings is...

_____

_____

_____

_____

_____

_____

_____

_____

_____

_____

_____

_____

His Memories of His Siblings

Another favorite memory of one or more of my siblings is...

_____

_____

_____

_____

_____

_____

_____

_____

_____

_____

_____

Another favorite memory of one or more of my siblings is...

_____

_____

_____

_____

_____

_____

_____

_____

_____

_____

_____

"You only live once, but if you do it right, once is enough."

– Mae West

Life Experiences

I Have...

	Grandmother	Grandfather
Flown in a plane.	☐	☐
Had surgery.	☐	☐
Been to a professional sporting event.	☐	☐
Been to the Empire State Building.	☐	☐
Run a marathon.	☐	☐
Made a speech in front of a large group.	☐	☐
Sung a solo in front of an audience.	☐	☐
Visited the Grand Canyon.	☐	☐
Gone on a cruise.	☐	☐
Had my tonsils removed.	☐	☐
Been in a band.	☐	☐
Seen the pyramids in Egypt.	☐	☐
Ridden in a hot air balloon.	☐	☐
Milked a cow.	☐	☐
Been to a Broadway musical	☐	☐
Driven on Route 66.	☐	☐
Learned a second language.	☐	☐
Ridden in a helicopter.	☐	☐
Met a celebrity.	☐	☐
Been to the Eiffel Tower.	☐	☐
Performed in a play or musical.	☐	☐
Ridden in a train.	☐	☐
Lived in a foreign country.	☐	☐
Been to the Golden Gate Bridge.	☐	☐
Gone snow skiing.	☐	☐
Flown a plane.	☐	☐
Attended the ballet.	☐	☐
Been to a Disney Park.	☐	☐
Gone bungee jumping.	☐	☐

	Grandmother	Grandfather
Been to Rome.	☐	☐
Seen a UFO.	☐	☐
Been a maid of honor/best man.	☐	☐
Been in a hurricane.	☐	☐
Gone deep sea fishing.	☐	☐
Been to a rodeo.	☐	☐
Been to Niagara Falls.	☐	☐
Seen a meteor shower.	☐	☐
Gone backpacking	☐	☐
Been selected for a jury.	☐	☐
Visited the Taj Mahal.	☐	☐
Ridden a horse.	☐	☐
Attended the opera.	☐	☐
Gone sailing.	☐	☐
Been to a tropical island.	☐	☐
Been on television.	☐	☐
Experienced an earthquake.	☐	☐
Traveled overseas.	☐	☐
Ridden in a gondola in Venice.	☐	☐
Gone ice skating.	☐	☐
Driven a tractor.	☐	☐
Gone skydiving.	☐	☐
Visited the Florida Keys.	☐	☐
Been a passenger in a private jet.	☐	☐
Gone scuba diving.	☐	☐
Been through a tornado storm.	☐	☐
Visited Las Vegas.	☐	☐
Gone surfing	☐	☐
Been on a safari.	☐	☐
Participated in a political protest.	☐	☐
Visited Washington D.C.	☐	☐
Ridden in a horse-drawn carriage.	☐	☐
Ridden a motorcycle.	☐	☐

"Before
I got married
I had
six theories
about
raising children;
now, I have
six children
and no theories."
– John Wilmot

Becoming a Parent

When We Became Parents

We were this age when we first became parents...

_____

_____

Our child's/children's names and dates of birth/adoption are...

_____

_____

_____

_____

_____

_____

_____

_____

_____

When We Became Parents

The stories of each of their births/adoptions are...

_____

_____

_____

_____

_____

_____

_____

_____

_____

_____

_____

_____

When We Became Parents

The stories of each of their births/adoptions are...

_____

_____

_____

_____

_____

_____

_____

_____

_____

_____

_____

_____

When We Became Parents

The stories of each of their births/adoptions are...

_____

_____

_____

_____

_____

_____

_____

_____

_____

_____

_____

_____

When We Became Parents

Our child's/children's' first words were...

_____

_____

_____

_____

_____

And they were these ages when they took their first steps...

_____

_____

_____

_____

_____

When We Became Parents

When they were little, I remember reading these books to them...

_____

_____

_____

_____

And singing these songs...

_____

_____

_____

_____

When they were upset, we would calm them by...

_____

_____

_____

_____

Her Memories of Becoming and Being a Mom

My favorite parts of being pregnant were...

_____

_____

_____

_____

And these were my least favorite parts...

_____

_____

_____

_____

My deliveries were premature/late/on-time...

_____

_____

_____

_____

Her Memories of Becoming and Being a Mom

I can remember having these food cravings during my pregnancies...

_____

_____

_____

_____

The story or a memory of our first child's first year of life is...

_____

_____

_____

_____

The story or a memory of our next child's first year of life is...

_____

_____

_____

_____

The story or a memory of our next child's first year of life is...

_____

_____

_____

_____

The story or a memory of our next child's first year of life is...

_____

_____

_____

_____

The story or a memory of our next child's first year of life is...

_____

_____

_____

_____

Her Memories of Becoming and Being a Mom

Based upon all I have experience and now know, this is the advice I would give myself as a new mother...

_____

_____

_____

_____

_____

_____

_____

_____

_____

_____

_____

_____

_____

A favorite memory of being a mother is...

_____

_____

_____

_____

_____

_____

Another favorite memory of being a mother is...

_____

_____

_____

_____

_____

_____

Another favorite memory of being a mother is...

_____

_____

_____

_____

_____

Another favorite memory of being a mother is...

_____

_____

_____

_____

_____

For me, the best and hardest parts of being a mother are...

_____

_____

_____

_____

_____

_____

_____

_____

_____

_____

_____

_____

Her Memories of Becoming and Being a Mom

In my opinion, the biggest differences in how kids are raised today and when I was young are...

_____

_____

_____

_____

_____

_____

_____

_____

_____

_____

_____

_____

The story or a memory of our first child's first year of life is...

_____

_____

_____

_____

The story or a memory of our next child's first year of life is...

_____

_____

_____

_____

The story or a memory of our next child's first year of life is...

_____

_____

_____

_____

His Memories of Becoming and Being a Dad

The story or a memory of our next child's first year of life is...

_____

_____

_____

_____

The story or a memory of our next child's first year of life is...

_____

_____

_____

_____

The story or a memory of our next child's first year of life is...

_____

_____

_____

_____

Based upon all I have experienced and now know, this is the advice I would give myself as a new father...

_____

_____

_____

_____

_____

_____

_____

_____

_____

_____

_____

_____

His Memories of Becoming and Being a Dad

A favorite memory of being a father is...

_____

_____

_____

_____

_____

_____

Another favorite memory of being a father is...

_____

_____

_____

_____

_____

_____

His Memories of Becoming and Being a Dad

Another favorite memory of being a father is...

_____

_____

_____

_____

_____

_____

Another favorite memory of being a father is...

_____

_____

_____

_____

_____

_____

His Memories of Becoming and Being a Dad

Another favorite memory of being a father is...

_____

_____

_____

_____

_____

_____

Another favorite memory of being a father is...

_____

_____

_____

_____

_____

_____

His Memories of Becoming and Being a Dad

For me, the best and hardest parts of being a father are...

_____

_____

_____

_____

_____

_____

_____

_____

_____

_____

_____

_____

_____

His Memories of Becoming and Being a Dad

In my opinion, the biggest differences in how kids are raised today and when
I was young are...

_____

_____

_____

_____

_____

_____

_____

_____

_____

_____

_____

_____

"Something magical happens when parents turn into grandparents."

– Author Unknown

Becoming a Grandparent

My Memories of
Becoming and Being a Grandmother

I was this age when I first became a grandparent...

_____

The first time I found out I was going to be a grandmother, I was told by...

_____

_____

This is how they told me...

_____

_____

_____

And this was my reaction...

_____

_____

_____

_____

My Memories of
Becoming and Being a Grandfather

I was this age when I first became a grandparent...

_____

The first time I found out I was going to be a grandfather, I was told by...

_____

_____

This is how they told me...

_____

_____

_____

_____

And this was my reaction...

_____

_____

_____

_____

My Memories of
Becoming and Being a Grandmother

In my opinion, the most surprising part of being a grandparent has been...

_____

_____

_____

_____

_____

And the biggest difference in being a grandmother instead of a mother is...

_____

_____

_____

_____

_____

My Memories of
Becoming and Being a Grandfather

In my opinion, the most surprising part of being a grandparent has been...

_____

_____

_____

_____

_____

And the biggest difference in being a grandfather instead of a father is...

_____

_____

_____

_____

_____

"Life
is not a
problem
to be solved,
but a reality
to be
experienced."
– Soren Kierkegaard

Things We Want to Do

Her List: 15 Things I Want to Do

1. _____

2. _____

3. _____

4. _____

5. _____

6. _____

7. _____

8. _____

9. _____

10. _____

11. _____

12. _____

13. _____

14. _____

15. _____

His List: 15 Things I Want to Do

1. _____

2. _____

3. _____

4. _____

5. _____

6. _____

7. _____

8. _____

9. _____

10. _____

11. _____

12. _____

13. _____

14. _____

15. _____

Her List: 15 Things I Want to Learn

1. _____

2. _____

3. _____

4. _____

5. _____

6. _____

7. _____

8. _____

9. _____

10. _____

11. _____

12. _____

13. _____

14. _____

15. _____

His List: 15 Things I Want to Learn

1. _____

2. _____

3. _____

4. _____

5. _____

6. _____

7. _____

8. _____

9. _____

10. _____

11. _____

12. _____

13. _____

14. _____

15. _____

Her List: 15 Places I Want to Travel To

1. _____

2. _____

3. _____

4. _____

5. _____

6. _____

7. _____

8. _____

9. _____

10. _____

11. _____

12. _____

13. _____

14. _____

15. _____

His List: 15 Places I Want to Travel To

1. _____

2. _____

3. _____

4. _____

5. _____

6. _____

7. _____

8. _____

9. _____

10. _____

11. _____

12. _____

13. _____

14. _____

15. _____

"In three words
I can sum up
everything
I've learned
about life:
It goes on."
– Robert Frost

Room for More

The pages in this section are for both of you to expand on some of your answers, share more memories, and/or to write notes to your loved ones:

_____

_____

_____

_____

_____

_____

_____

_____

_____

_____

_____

The pages in this section are for both of you to expand on some of your answers, share more memories, and/or to write notes to your loved ones:

_____

_____

_____

_____

_____

_____

_____

_____

_____

_____

_____

_____

The pages in this section are for both of you to expand on some of your answers, share more memories, and/or to write notes to your loved ones:

_____

_____

_____

_____

_____

_____

_____

_____

_____

_____

_____

_____

The pages in this section are for both of you to expand on some of your answers, share more memories, and/or to write notes to your loved ones:

_____

_____

_____

_____

_____

_____

_____

_____

_____

_____

_____

_____

_____

_____

The pages in this section are for both of you to expand on some of your answers, share more memories, and/or to write notes to your loved ones:

_____

_____

_____

_____

_____

_____

_____

_____

_____

_____

_____

The pages in this section are for both of you to expand on some of your answers, share more memories, and/or to write notes to your loved ones:

_____

_____

_____

_____

_____

_____

_____

_____

_____

_____

_____

_____

_____

The pages in this section are for both of you to expand on some of your answers, share more memories, and/or to write notes to your loved ones:

_____

_____

_____

_____

_____

_____

_____

_____

_____

_____

_____

_____

The pages in this section are for both of you to expand on some of your answers, share more memories, and/or to write notes to your loved ones:

_____

_____

_____

_____

_____

_____

_____

_____

_____

_____

_____

_____

The pages in this section are for both of you to expand on some of your answers, share more memories, and/or to write notes to your loved ones:

_____

_____

_____

_____

_____

_____

_____

_____

_____

_____

_____

The pages in this section are for both of you to expand on some of your answers, share more memories, and/or to write notes to your loved ones:

_____

_____

_____

_____

_____

_____

_____

_____

_____

_____

_____

_____

_____

The pages in this section are for both of you to expand on some of your answers, share more memories, and/or to write notes to your loved ones:

_____

_____

_____

_____

_____

_____

_____

_____

_____

_____

_____

_____

The pages in this section are for both of you to expand on some of your answers, share more memories, and/or to write notes to your loved ones:

_____

_____

_____

_____

_____

_____

_____

_____

_____

_____

_____

_____

_____

The pages in this section are for both of you to expand on some of your answers, share more memories, and/or to write notes to your loved ones:

The pages in this section are for both of you to expand on some of your answers, share more memories, and/or to write notes to your loved ones:

_____

_____

_____

_____

_____

_____

_____

_____

_____

_____

_____

_____

The pages in this section are for both of you to expand on some of your answers, share more memories, and/or to write notes to your loved ones:

_____

_____

_____

_____

_____

_____

_____

_____

_____

_____

_____

_____

_____

The pages in this section are for both of you to expand on some of your answers, share more memories, and/or to write notes to your loved ones:

_____

_____

_____

_____

_____

_____

_____

_____

_____

_____

_____

_____

Hear Your Story Books

At **Hear Your Story**, we have created a line of books focused on giving each of us a place to tell the unique story of who we are, where we have been, and where we are going.

Sharing and hearing the stories of the people in our lives creates a closeness and understanding, ultimately strengthening our bonds.

Available at Amazon, all bookstores, and HearYourStoryBooks.com

- Mom, I Want to Hear Your Story: A Mother's Guided Journal to Share Her Life & Her Love

- Dad, I Want to Hear Your Story: A Father's Guided Journal to Share His Life & His Love

- Life Gave Me You; I Want to Hear Your Story: A Guided Journal for Stepmothers to Share Their Life Story

- You Choose to Be My Dad; I Want to Hear Your Story: A Guided Journal for Stepdads to Share Their Life Story

- To My Wonderful Aunt, I Want to Hear Your Story: A Guided Journal to Share Her Life and Her Love

- To My Uncle, I Want to Hear Your Story: A Guided Journal to Share His Life and His Love

- Mom, I Want to Learn Your Recipes: A Keepsake Memory Book to Gather and Preserve Your Favorite Family Recipes

- Grandmother, I Want to Learn Your Recipes: A Keepsake Memory Book to Gather and Preserve Your Favorite Family Recipes

- Aunt, I Want to Learn Your Recipes: A Keepsake Memory Book to Gather and Preserve Your Favorite Family Recipes
- Dad, I Want to Learn Your Recipes: A Keepsake Memory Book to Gather and Preserve Your Favorite Family Recipes
- Mom & Me: Let's Learn Together Journal for Kids
- The Story of Expecting You: A Self-care Pregnancy Guided Journal and Memory Book
- To My Girlfriend, I Want to Hear Your Story
- To My Boyfriend, I Want to Hear Your Story

About the Author

Jeffrey Mason is the creator and author of the best-selling **Hear Your Story®** line of books and is the founder of the company **Hear Your Story®**.

In response to his own father's fight with Alzheimer's, Jeffrey wrote his first two books, **Mom, I Want to Hear Your Story** and **Dad, I Want to Hear Your Story** in 2019. Since then, he has written and designed over 30 books, been published in four languages, and sold over 300,000 copies worldwide.

Jeffrey is dedicated to spreading the mission that the little things are the big things and that each of us has an incredible life story that needs to be shared and celebrated. He continues to create books that he hopes will guide people to reflect on and share their full life experience, while creating opportunities for talking, listening, learning, and understanding.

Hear Your Story® can be visited at **hearyourstorybooks.com** and Jeffrey can be contacted for questions, comments, podcasting, speaking engagements, or just a hello at **jeffrey.mason@hearyourstory.com**.

He would be grateful if you would help people find his books by leaving a review on Amazon. Your feedback helps him get better at this thing he loves.

We invite you to also check out HearYourStory.com,
where you can answer the questions in this book using your
smart phone, tablet, or computer.

Answering the questions online at HearYourStory.com allows
you to write as much as you want, to save your responses and revisit
and revise them whenever you wish, and to print as many copies as you
need for you and your whole family.

Please note there is a small one-time charge
to cover the cost of maintaining the site.

Made in the USA
Las Vegas, NV
29 October 2023

79829539R00168